The Smithsonian

MUSEUMS OF THE WORLD

By Megan Kopp

MEDIA ENHANCED BOOKS
AV2
BY WEIGL™
ADDED VALUE • AUDIO VISUAL

www.av2books.com

AV² provides enriched content that supplements and complements this book. Weigl's AV² books strive to create inspired learning and engage young minds in a total learning experience.

Your AV² Media Enhanced books come alive with...

Audio
Listen to sections of the book read aloud.

Key Words
Study vocabulary, and complete a matching word activity.

Go to **www.av2books.com,** and enter this book's unique code.

Video
Watch informative video clips.

Quizzes
Test your knowledge.

BOOK CODE

W933636

Embedded Weblinks
Gain additional information for research.

Slide Show
View images and captions, and prepare a presentation.

AV² by Weigl brings you media enhanced books that support active learning.

Try This!
Complete activities and hands-on experiments.

... and much, much more!

Published by AV² by Weigl
350 5th Avenue, 59th Floor
New York, NY 10118
Websites: www.av2books.com www.weigl.com

Editor: Heather Kissock
Design: Dean Pickup

Every reasonable effort has been made to trace ownership and to obtain permission to reprint copyright material. The publishers would be pleased to have any errors or omissions brought to their attention so that they may be corrected in subsequent printings.

Weigl acknowledges Getty Images, Alamy, Newscom, and Dreamstime as its primary image suppliers for this title.

Library of Congress Cataloging-in-Publication Data
Kopp, Megan.
The Smithsonian / Megan Kopp.
     pages cm. -- (Museums of the world)
Includes index.
 ISBN 978-1-4896-1198-7 (hardcover : alk. paper) -- ISBN 978-1-4896-1199-4 (softcover : alk. paper) --
ISBN 978-1-4896-1200-7 (single user ebk.) -- ISBN 978-1-4896-1201-4 (multi user ebk.)
 1. Smithsonian Institution. 2. Museums--United States. I. Title.
 Q11.S8K67 2015
 069.09753--dc23
                           2014006383
Printed in the United States of America in North Mankato, Minnesota
1 2 3 4 5 6 7 8 9 0 18 17 16 15 14

032014
WEP150314

Contents

What Is the Smithsonian?

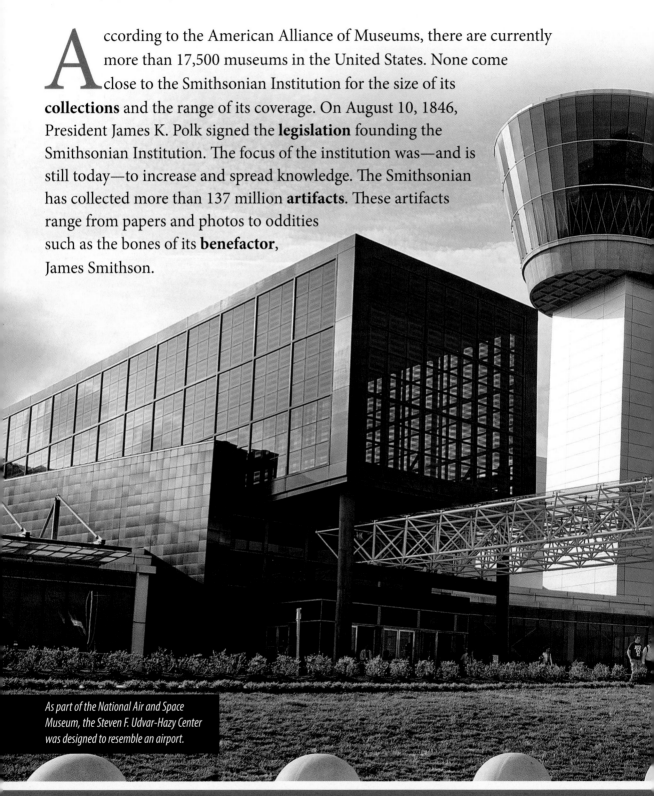

According to the American Alliance of Museums, there are currently more than 17,500 museums in the United States. None come close to the Smithsonian Institution for the size of its **collections** and the range of its coverage. On August 10, 1846, President James K. Polk signed the **legislation** founding the Smithsonian Institution. The focus of the institution was—and is still today—to increase and spread knowledge. The Smithsonian has collected more than 137 million **artifacts**. These artifacts range from papers and photos to oddities such as the bones of its **benefactor**, James Smithson.

As part of the National Air and Space Museum, the Steven F. Udvar-Hazy Center was designed to resemble an airport.

The Smithsonian Institution consists of 19 different museums and galleries, 20 libraries, nine research centers, and one zoo. These institutions are located mainly in Washington, DC. However, the Smithsonian also has two museums in New York City. The museums in the Washington, DC area include the National Museum of African Art, the National Air and Space Museum, the National Museum of the American Indian, and the National Postal Museum. The National Museum of the American Indian George Gustav Heye Center and the Cooper-Hewitt National Design Museum are the two museums located in New York City.

30 million people
visited Smithsonian museums in 2013.

James Smithson,
the institution's founder,
never set foot in the United States.

The Smithsonian's National Air and Space Museum is the

most visited museum in the country.

There is
NO ENTRY FEE
for any of the Smithsonian's museums in Washington, DC.

The Smithsonian has
more than 6,000
permanent staff members
and almost as many volunteers.

History of the Smithsonian

The Smithsonian Institution was founded under curious circumstances. When British scientist James Smithson died, his will left more than $500,000 to the United States, even though Smithson had no known connection to the country. The will stipulated that the money be put toward the creation of an institution that would foster learning. The U.S. government wanted to make sure that it used the money in an effective way, and a debate began to determine the best way to meet the conditions of the will. After eight years of discussion, the Smithsonian Institution was established.

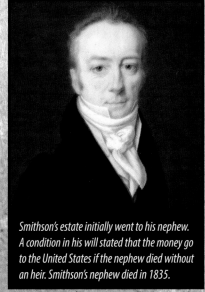

Smithson's estate initially went to his nephew. A condition in his will stated that the money go to the United States if the nephew died without an heir. Smithson's nephew died in 1835.

1846 Legislation is passed in Congress, founding the Smithsonian Institution.

1881 The first United States National Museum, now known as the Arts and Industries Building, opens in Washington, DC. It houses the collections once displayed in the Smithsonian Institution Building.

1825   **1850**   **1875**   **1900**

1836 The U.S. government inherits Smithson's estate. A committee is set up to determine the best way to spend the money.

1855 The Smithsonian Institution Building is completed and opens to the public.

1910 A new National Museum opens on Washington's National Mall, providing the space required for the Smithsonian's growing collection.

The original Smithsonian Institution Building is also called The Castle because of its castle-like appearance.

1964 The National Museum of American History becomes the sixth Smithsonian building on the National Mall in Washington, DC.

1976 The National Air and Space Museum joins the other Smithsonian buildings on the National Mall.

1950   1975   2000   2025

1968 The Smithsonian continues to expand, opening its American Art Museum and National Portrait Gallery in Washington's historic Patent Office.

1993 The National Postal Museum opens it doors.

2012 The space shuttle *Discovery* finds a permanent home at the National Air and Space Museum's Steven F. Udvar-Hazy Center.

Key People

The Smithsonian came to be through the vision and dedication of a number of people. The people initially involved in the institution's development worked with only a vague concept about a place of learning. These people provided the push needed to keep the project moving forward. As the concept became clearer, people with specific expertise were brought in to make the museum a reality.

James Smithson (1765–1829)

James Smithson was born in France in 1765, but became a British citizen at the age of 10. His interest in science led him to Pembroke College. Upon graduating, he quickly established himself as a chemist and mineralogist. Over the course of his life, he published 27 scientific papers and had a mineral called smithsonite named in his honor. Smithson never married. When he died in Genoa, Italy, on June 27, 1829, he was buried in a local cemetery. His body was later moved to The Castle at the Smithsonian Institution.

James Smithson's wealth came from his mother's side of the family. His mother had links to the British royal family.

Richard Rush (1780–1859)

Even though Smithson's estate was to go to the United States after his nephew's death, the process did not go smoothly. The mother of Smithson's nephew went to court and filed a claim for the money. The U.S. government sent Philadelphia lawyer Richard Rush to London to argue its case. Rush came from a prominent American family. He graduated from Princeton University at the age of 17 and was practicing law within three years. In 1814, he became the U.S. attorney general. His knowledge of law and his skill as a diplomat were useful in negotiating the Smithson bequest. Rush was able to secure the funds for the United States within two years.

Richard Rush was the son of Benjamin Rush, one of the signers of the Declaration of Independence.

James Renwick, Jr. (1818–1895)

Architect James Renwick, Jr. won the competition for the design of the Smithsonian Institution Building in 1846. Renwick's design was a mix of different architectural styles that were popular in medieval Europe. Renwick was one of the country's top architects at the time. Born in New York City, he graduated from Columbia College at the age of 21 with a Master of Arts degree. He then embarked on a career as an engineer but later turned to architecture. Prior to winning the contract for the Smithsonian Institution Building, he was best known for designing churches. Following the Smithsonian project, he returned to church design, drawing up the plans for one of the county's best-known churches, St. Patrick's Cathedral, in New York City.

James Renwick, Jr. later designed another Smithsonian building, the Renwick Gallery, which is part of the American Art Museum.

Joseph Henry (1797–1878)

Joseph Henry became the Smithsonian Institution's first secretary on December 3, 1846. As secretary, he was responsible for setting out a guiding plan for the institution's direction. At the time of his hiring, Henry was best known as a physicist and professor. Henry was born in Albany, New York. His family was not wealthy, and Henry had to work hard to obtain an education. He only began attending the Albany Academy at the age of 21. He later became a professor at the school. In 1832, he became a professor of natural philosophy at New Jersey College, which is now known as Princeton University.

Joseph Henry was known around the world for his research in electromagnetism.

The Smithsonian Today

The Smithsonian Institution has experienced much development since its early years and is now considered the world's largest museum and research complex. The Smithsonian's museums cover a significant portion of Washington's National Mall, and the institution itself has locations and **affiliate** partners in other states across the country. The Smithsonian has also reached outside the United States to form partnerships with museums around the world. In doing so, it is fulfilling its vision to shape the future by preserving history, discovering new knowledge, and sharing information.

The Museo Alameda was the first affiliate museum of the Smithsonian. Located in San Antonio, Texas, the museum celebrated the Latino experience.

National Museum of the American Indian

The artifacts in this museum provide a look into the native peoples of the western hemisphere.

National Air and Space Museum

Showcasing America's contributions to flight, this museum features 23 galleries of aircraft and spacecraft.

Hirshhorn Museum

Art from modern masters and emerging artists is on display at the Hirshhorn.

The Castle

The original building now serves as an information and administrative center.

National Museum of Natural History

This green-domed museum explores the history of Earth from prehistoric times to the present.

National Museum of American History

With more than 3 million artifacts, **exhibits** in the National Museum of American History explore major themes in U.S. history and culture.

Touring the Smithsonian

The Smithsonian offers visitors a diverse range of experiences. Art, history, culture, and technology are all given their individual space while still remaining part of the larger institution. The scope of the Smithsonian's museums allows the institution to foster a love of learning in its guests.

National Air and Space Museum

The National Air and Space Museum has the world's largest collection of aviation and space artifacts. The museum has two parts. The museum proper is located on the National Mall, while the open, hangar-like Steven F. Udvar-Hazy Center is found near Washington Dulles International Airport.

The National Air and Space Museum has approximately 60,000 items in its collection.

The William H. Gross Stamp Gallery is the world's largest exhibition space devoted to stamp collection.

National Postal Museum

The National Postal Museum has five exhibition galleries devoted to postal history and philately, or stamp collecting. The newest exhibit space, the William H. Gross Stamp Gallery, opened in 2013. Here, visitors can see the world's first postage stamp, the 1840 Penny Black picturing a young Queen Victoria.

National Museum of the American Indian This museum pays tribute to native groups throughout the Americas. It has three main galleries, each focusing on a different aspect of American Indian life. Space is also allotted to traveling exhibits.

Visitors to the National Museum of the American Indian can watch Aboriginal artists creating traditional art.

Natural History Museum From prehistoric creatures to world cultures, the Natural History Museum provides visitors with a history of the world. The museum even features a morphing station where visitors can see themselves as early humans.

The Mammal Hall exhibits show how animals from around the world have adapted to their environment.

The National Air and Space Museum is the **largest of the 19 Smithsonian museums.**

Approximately **4 million people visit** the American History Museum every year.

The National Museum of the American Indian represents more than **1,200 cultural groups** from across the Americas.

The Natural History Museum covers **18 football fields** of space.

The National Zoological Park features **400 of the world's animal species,**

1/4 of which are endangered.

The Air and
Space Museum has

more than 400 artifacts

from the *Apollo 11* Moon landing.

More than 12,000 years

of Aboriginal life are on display
at the American Indian Museum.

Size 5

The ruby red shoes Judy Garland wore in

The Wizard of Oz,

now on display at the
American History Museum.

66 million years old

The age of the

7-ton

Tyrannosaurus rex fossil at the Natural
History Museum. (6.4 metric tons)

The National Portrait Gallery has

the only complete collection

of presidential portraits
outside of the White House.

Treasures of the Smithsonian

The Smithsonian is an American institution. Many of its artifacts represent key people and moments in American history. However, the Smithsonian also has strong links to the international community. Over the years, it has acquired objects that have deep meaning not only to the people of the United States, but people from around the world.

The 1903 Wright Flyer, on display at the National Air and Space Museum, was the world's first successful airplane.

The command module served as the cabin for a 3-person crew.

Skylab 4 Command Module The "Apollo to the Moon" exhibit at the National Air and Space Museum features the Skylab 4 command **module**. The module was used to take astronauts to and from Skylab, America's first space station. Skylab 4 was the final mission to the space station. The astronauts lived in the module for 84 days and performed several experiments.

Star-Spangled Banner The Star-Spangled Banner is one of the National Museum of American History's best-known artifacts. This flag was raised over Fort McHenry after the United States won a key battle over Great Britain in the **War of 1812**. The wool and cotton flag measures 30 by 34 feet (9.1 by 10.4 m).

The Star-Spangled Banner celebrated its 200th birthday in 2014.

The Hope Diamond was shipped to the Smithsonian by mail. It arrived in a box wrapped in brown paper.

Hope Diamond The National Museum of Natural History is home to the Hope Diamond. The 45.52-carat gemstone is the largest deep-blue diamond in the world. Before arriving at the Smithsonian, it was owned by kings of France, a British lord, and famed jeweller Pierre Cartier. It is estimated to be worth about $350 million.

Postcard from Space Space mail hit the headlines on August 2, 1971, when U.S. astronaut Dave Scott postmarked an envelope on the Moon. The envelope, complete with smudges from Scott's spacesuit glove, can be seen in the Smithsonian's National Postal Museum.

Scott's envelope holds two postmarks. The first one was faint, so Scott stamped the paper again.

Collection Conservation

The Smithsonian's art and artifacts are vulnerable to a number of conditions. Damage can come from too much sunlight, not enough moisture, insects, chips, and dents. **Conservators** work to prevent these and many other potential threats to the artifacts. The Smithsonian's museums have a dedicated team of conservators who work to preserve and protect the institution's collections. They are assisted by the Smithsonian Conservation Institute, which works to develop new conservation techniques for the collections.

Filling in the Picture Conservators work to restore paintings to a condition that closely resembles an earlier or undamaged state. To clean a painting, the conservator carefully removes layers of grime and varnish that have darkened the painting over time. Areas of lost paint can be filled in with a **primer** and then painted to match the surrounding areas of original paint.

Before going on display, paintings are assessed, and any needed restoration work is done.

Light Works In partnership with SOLEIL Synchrotron of France, the Smithsonian is using synchrotron technology to study and preserve its collections. The synchrotron creates extremely bright, stable light that allows scientists to observe matter down to individual atoms. This helps conservators learn more about the way materials react in certain conditions. They can then develop conservation techniques for those materials.

Synchrotron technology can be used to find hidden paintings underneath the existing artwork.

In the Lunder Conservation Center, on the fourth floor of the American Art Museum, visitors can see conservators work in five different labs and studios.

Keeping It Cold

Over time, most materials experience deterioration. Rubber, for instance, **oxidizes**. Conservators have discovered that rubber can be preserved against chemical breakdown using cold storage. This technique does make the rubber more brittle, but this loss of elasticity is reversed when the material is returned to room temperature. Cold storage is a good tool for long-term preservation.

To protect the rubber inside, spacesuits are usually stored in a cool, dry environment.

Mold Matters

Too much moisture can lead to the development of mold. Catching mold before it damages artifacts is important. Ultraviolet (UV) light, or "black light", shows changes in the makeup of the surface of objects. Mold is often apparent in UV light even when it is completely invisible in normal light. Early detection allows conservators to remove the mold before the artifact is irreversibly damaged.

Conservators use ultraviolet torches to detect imperfections and previous restoration attempts.

The Smithsonian in the World

From its early years, the Smithsonian Institute has been focused on sharing knowledge. Today, the Smithsonian has a variety of programs and media designed to share its resources with the world. Some of the methods used are traditional in nature. Others take advantages of advances in technology.

Mobile Apps The Smithsonian offers 30 mobile apps that allow people to access its wealth of information. Some apps help visitors find their way around a museum. Others give overviews of specific exhibits. Smithsonian podcasts, documentaries, and games are also available through the institution's various apps.

Most of the Smithsonian's apps were created after consulting with museum visitors.

Publications As an institution of learning, the Smithsonian is active in publishing research and technical papers from its experts. These articles often appear in **academic journals**. However, the Smithsonian also publishes nonfiction books and a general interest magazine that are meant to reach a wider audience of both adults and children alike. These publications cover a range of topics, including science, history, technology, and art.

Smithsonian publications are sold in the museum's bookstores and in bookstores around the world.

Traveling Exhibits

Traveling exhibits allow people in faraway places to experience the Smithsonian. The Smithsonian Institution Traveling Exhibition Service (SITES) creates exhibits that follow a specific theme. Items from their collections, display cases, and related brochures are gathered into a package that is made available to museums, libraries, science centers, and even shopping malls. Since its creation in 1951, SITES has put together more than 1,500 exhibits.

Exhibits are sometimes placed in non-traditional locations to reach a wider audience.

Education Programs

The Smithsonian has a number of programs designed for classroom use. The institution provides learning opportunities for both teachers and students. Teachers can benefit from the Smithsonian's workshops and teaching packages. The Smithsonian also offers video conferences with expert guest speakers. As with most museums, the Smithsonian helps teachers arrange field trips that touch on subjects being taught in their classrooms. Online databases allow learners of all ages to access information on a variety of topics.

The Smithsonian's annual Folklife Festival is an informal education program that allows people to learn about other cultures. Presentations feature the music, food, dance, and crafts of various ethnic groups.

Looking to the Future

The Smithsonian continues to develop its online presence. It has been gradually **digitizing** its collection for online use. However, this project will take years to complete due to the large number of items the institution holds. The Smithsonian recently unveiled three-dimensional (3-D) imaging technology. This allows objects to be viewed online from the back, front, and sides. People will soon be able to view an object as they would if they were in the museum.

In 2015, a new museum will join the Smithsonian's list of attractions. The National Museum of African American History and Culture will open on Washington's National Mall. This museum will showcase the contributions African Americans have made to the United States throughout its history.

Digitizing the collections allows people to visit the Smithsonian from home.

President Obama spoke at the groundbreaking ceremony for the National Museum of African American History and Culture in 2012.

NATIONAL MUSEUM OF AFRICAN AMERICAN HISTORY AND CULTURE

Smithsonian
NATIONAL MUSEUM
AFRICAN AMERIC

Activity

The Smithsonian Institution brings together a group of museums. Each has a unique theme or focus. With such a wide variety of subjects to explore, the Smithsonian meets the interests of a large audience. Think about the museums, research centers, and zoo that make up the Smithsonian. Which one interests you the most?

Imagine that you are a tour guide for this museum, research center, or zoo. Follow these steps to plan a tour that will show visitors the site's most important items.

You will need: a computer and printer, a pen, paper, glue, bristol board, and scissors.

1. Research online to determine which parts of the collection you should show visitors.

2. Read the descriptions of each item, and write down any details you would want to share with your tour group.

3. Using your printer, print a picture of each item you want to discuss. Cut out the pictures.

4. Write the name of your museum at the top of the bristol board. Paste your pictures to the bristol board in the order in which you would show them to your tour group. Draw arrows between the objects to show the path you would take.

5. Use your tour map to take your class or friends on your tour. Remember to tell them something interesting about each piece you are presenting.

Smithsonian Quiz

1 Who was the Smithsonian's benefactor?

2 In what year was the Smithsonian founded?

3 What is the Smithsonian's first building often called?

4 What is the main goal of the Smithsonian Institution?

5 How many museums and galleries does the Smithsonian have?

ANSWERS:

1. James Smithson
2. 1846
3. The Castle
4. To increase and spread knowledge
5. 19

Key Words

academic journals: publications that contains scholarly articles

affiliate: an organization officially connected to a larger body

artifacts: objects from the past

benefactor: a financial supporter

collections: works of art or other items collected for exhibit and study in a museum, and kept as part of its holdings

conservators: people who protect objects from deterioration

digitizing: converting pictures into a digital form that can be processed by a computer

exhibits: displays of objects or artwork within a theme

legislation: the making of laws

module: part of a space vehicle

oxidizes: combines a substance with oxygen, causing it to change form

primer: an undercoat of paint used to prepare a painting surface

War of 1812: a war between the United States and Great Britain that lasted from 1812 to 1815

Index

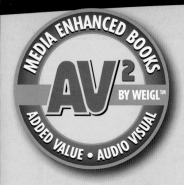

Log on to www.av2books.com

AV² by Weigl brings you media enhanced books that support active learning. Go to www.av2books.com, and enter the special code found on page 2 of this book. You will gain access to enriched and enhanced content that supplements and complements this book. Content includes video, audio, weblinks, quizzes, a slide show, and activities.

AV² Online Navigation

Book Pages
AV² pages directly correspond to pages in the book.

Audio
Listen to sections of the book read aloud.

Video
Watch informative video clips.

Embedded Weblinks
Gain additional information for research.

Try This!
Complete activities and hands-on experiments.

Key Words
Study vocabulary, and complete a matching word activity.

Quizzes
Test your knowledge.

Slide Show
View images and captions, and prepare a presentation.

AV² was built to bridge the gap between print and digital. We encourage you to tell us what you like and what you want to see in the future.

Sign up to be an AV² Ambassador at www.av2books.com/ambassador.